Cover design: Daniel Añez
Cover and interior illustrations: GettyImages.com
Interior design: Aaron Troia

Copyright © 2023 by Pacific Press® Publishing Association
Printed in China
All rights reserved

To order additional copies of this book, call toll-free 1–800-765–6955 or visit AdventistBookCenter.com.

ISBN 978-0-8163-6957-7

August 2023

Contents

KarrLayn Beck

One phone call. And our lives would be forever changed.
On December 10, 2017, while prepping for the arrival of thirty festive friends for our annual staff Christmas party, my vacuuming stopped. "It's Brandon," my wife Cherié said, handing me the phone. "They found a tumor in KarrLayn's liver. That's why she was so sick on Thanksgiving."

It felt like a baseball bat to my throat. I sat, too stunned to breathe.

Cherié finally snapped the silence. "Karl, would you pray while we still got Brandon on the phone?"

"Huh? . . . Oh, um, yeah, yeah, sure."

The following ten months remain a thick smog. Chemo options, the kids, fits of rage, conversations about heaven and popcorn and macchiatos, watching family videos, our escape to Sunriver for two days, hospice, heaven, hate, hope, health—the snapshots are random and blurry at best.

Our fiercest impulse was to help. To research treatment options. To be there when they wheeled her out of surgery. To manage the myriad of visitors. To drop hope into the dismal decline we couldn't deny as the cancer drained her spunk and vigor.

Our main contribution in the hope department came by way of sending KarrLayn texts from "The Haff Version" of the Bible. Admittedly, this is not a legitimate translation of Scripture; rather, it's our informal and creative attempt at putting the grand promises of God into language that speaks to our real lives, as messy as they may be.

There was one thing we could count on. Within minutes of sending a fresh paraphrase, we would receive a response from KarrLayn. Now we treasure her texts in ways we never could have imagined. Here are a few of her replies

- "Karl and Lindsey, I am in tears. I love this. I have been a bit low this week, so it is especially meaningful. Thanks for sharing just now!" (Her reply to our paraphrase of Isaiah 43:1–3).
- "Wow!!! That is really boosting! Sounds like it's written just for me. Thank you. Sitting here waiting for my first appointment" (2 Corinthians 4:16–18).
- "Some day you must share your paraphrases in

a book for others who are going through tough times. These paraphrases are really blessing and encouraging me. You have no idea how meaningful these are" (Romans 5:1–5).

- "Thank you for all the prayers. This is really good. I like the idea of paying hope forward" (2 Corinthians 1:3, 4).

- "Thank you, Karl and Lindsey! I was having a discouraging moment, frustration with the treatments changing and trying to schedule the treatments etc. Your text came at the perfect time and was a gift to be reminded that God will see me [us] thru. Thank you, thank you, thank you!" (Isaiah 41:10–13).

- "That's a great perspective! I am alive now, and I will praise him for each step he leads me through this hellish journey, as he guides me closer to heaven" (Isaiah 38:16–19).

- "I really enjoy these paraphrases. I look each one up in the Bible on my phone because I usually don't recognize them. But the message is the same. —They are so personable, like God is sending a letter just for me. I love it! Thank you, Karl and Lindsey, for including me in the process. They are so helpful. I know they will touch many hearts!"

In whatever way our paraphrases were helpful to Karr-Layn, the practice was most helpful to us as well. This process of rewording God's Word into our everyday words proved healing for us during the dark days of saying good-bye. In addition to our Haff Version paraphrase, each chapter includes a brief story, a few Bible verses from a variety of translations, some quotes, and room for your reflections.

Perhaps this practice of paraphrasing the promises of God will prove helpful to you as well. To this end, you will find space to journal. You may wish to write a short note to God, paraphrase your own Bible verse, or jot down what you're feeling. In whatever way you choose to make Scripture personal and relevant, we want you to feel God weighing in when life weighs you down.

CHAPTER 1

God Reminding You

Stay strong!
Be brave!
No fear.
Don't let the enemy intimidate you.
I am with you.
As close as your breath.
Trust Me. I will not forsake you. I will not fail you.
Nothing will happen today that we can't tackle
*   together.*
                    —God (Deuteronomy 31:6, The Haff Version)

Whatever challenge you are facing, never forget that God is with you. Even when you shun Him, He pursues you. Never lose the deep confidence that no matter how severe the circumstances, God is always nearby. As this adapted version of C. V. Garnett's story reminds us, there is no way to escape the presence of God.

It was a hot sticky night in Miami. Brad could feel the heat rising from the sidewalk as he ambled down Biscayne Boulevard. Cars whizzed past, people walked past, sirens wailed past. But Brad did not care for any of it. He just wanted to be by himself. If only he could be alone, to pray aloud.

Sometimes silent prayer will not do. There are times when a man needs to hear the sound of his own voice reverberating to God. *If only there was a wayside chapel*, Brad thought, *or a church that was open.*

He kept walking. Then he saw it. He could hardly believe it, but there it was—a lovely glass door opened into a dimly lit chapel. Small wooden pews, a tiny altar, soft lighting. Perfect. Next to the door hung a sign: Come in, You're Welcome to Sit, Pray, Meditate, or Eat Your Lunch.

By the entrance, Brad noticed a podium holding a guest book. It had columns for names, addresses, and comments. People from numerous states had autographed the book. In the comment column some had left statements: "Praise the Lord" or "Jesus saves" or "I have found Him here!" Many expressed praise for the very existence of such a place. Brad wrote a note expressing his good fortune in finding the place.

Then the page blew back, and one statement caught his eye.

In neat penmanship were these poignant words: "Gail was here but left for good."

A pathetic statement. At best a flippant, feeble joke. At worst the sincere cry of a desperate soul. Either way, Brad thought it tragic, for it revealed a person who was disillusioned, a person who felt rejected by God.

The words stung Brad. So much so that when he seated himself in the rough-hewn pew he could think of nothing else. His own problems took a back seat to Gail's.

The prayers Brad longed to pray for himself were superseded. At that moment, Gail and her soul became his primary concern. He prayed that God might reach down and save Gail.

With reluctance, Brad left the sacred ground he'd just found. The space provided a quiet haven; and in that haven, peace.

A few blocks from the chapel, a thought struck Brad. He turned and raced back.

Gail would hardly be there tonight. She had, after all, recorded that she would never return. Still . . . she might come back, sometime. The Spirit of the Lord could, in answer to Brad's own prayer, call her back for an unscheduled visit. And if so, she must know that someone cared. That, indeed, God cared.

Breathless, Brad opened the glass door and stepped inside the chapel. It was still empty. He turned to the visitor's book and picked up the pen. In the column beside the words "Gail was here but left for good," he wrote, "God was here but left for Gail."[1]

Whatever season of struggle you find yourself in, remember that God is with you.

"Be strong and of a good courage, fear not, nor be afraid of them: for the LORD thy God, he it is that doth go with thee; he will not fail thee, nor forsake thee" (Deuteronomy 31:6).

"You will show me the way of life, granting me the joy of your presence and the pleasures of living with you forever" (Psalm 16:11, NLT).

"The Eternal your God is standing right here among
        you,
    and He is the champion who will rescue you.
He will joyfully celebrate over you;
    He will rest in His love *for you*; He will joyfully sing
        because of you *like a new husband*" (Zephaniah
        3:17, VOICE).

"Certainly, for those who belong to the Lord and follow Him, He is with us in times of distress, and that is a comforting truth, but He wants to be part of every experience and every moment of our lives, because the human race will always be in need of a Savior."

—Billy Graham

"God, who is everywhere, never leaves us. Yet He seems sometimes to be present, sometimes absent. If we do not know Him well, we do not realize that He may be more present to us when He is absent than when He is present."

—Thomas Merton, *No Man Is an Island*

"I felt God coming back to me, and then I realized it was me coming back to Him and He had never left. The absence of God is an illusion I construct so the distance between us can be His fault rather than mine. His love is constant. Mine is not. He is HERE. Where am I?"

—Ty Gibson

"If we must 'feel' God's presence before we believe he is with us, we again reduce God to our ability to grasp him, making him an idol instead of acknowledging him as God."

—Craig S. Keener, *Gift and Giver: The Holy Spirit for Today*

"We may ignore, but we can nowhere evade, the presence of God. The World is crowded with Him. He walks everywhere *incognito*."

—C. S. Lewis

"Wide awake to the presence of God, I realized I had been so focused on asking why a good God allowed bad things to happen that I was missing out on the nearness of God all along. In becoming preoccupied with the why, I was missing the who."

—Margaret Feinberg

1. C. V. Garnett, "All the Way Back," in *Insight's Most Unforgettable Stories*, ed. Chris Blake (Hagerstown, MD: Review and Herald®, 1990), 182–184.

Greetings, God

Here's what I'm thinking:

Here's what I'm feeling:

Here's how we can do this together:

Know I am with you,
and I will watch over
you no matter where
you go."

—Genesis 28:15, VOICE

CHAPTER 2

Defining Commands From God

Be . . .

Strong, *adj.*, exerting great power; vigorous or robust: *a strong heart.*

Bold, *adj.*, not hesitating or fearful in the face of danger; courageous and daring: *She was bold—undaunted by the grim diagnosis.*

Fearless, *adj.*, without fear; brave; intrepid: *He showed fearless resolve during the experimental treatments.*

Encouraged, *past part.*, to receive support, confidence, or hope: *Your heavenly Father wants you to be encouraged, for He is in your corner.*

"Wherever you go, whatever you face, whenever you wonder . . . know this: I am with you.

"Always."

—God (Joshua 1:9, The Haff Version)

Next time you feel overwhelmed and you are paralyzed from pressing forward, recite Olivia's prayer. As a young girl, Olivia was afraid to walk to her grandpa's house next door because it involved going through a field of tall grass. She was frightened because of the "monsters and boogiemen" rumored to lurk there.

Her father assured her that God would go with her. "Don't fear," he said, "Jesus is a real friend. You won't be alone. He's with you all the time—even in that scary field."

"Really?" Olivia wanted to be sure.

"Yes, He really is."

Suddenly she perked up. "Okay, then. I'm going to Grandpa's . . . Come on Jesus."

Next time you're afraid to step forward in faith, pray that prayer, "Come on Jesus." He promises to hold your hand.

"Have not I commanded thee? Be strong and of a good courage; be not afraid, neither be thou dismayed: for the LORD thy God is with thee whithersoever thou goest" (Joshua 1:9).

"If your heart is broken, you'll find GOD right there; if you're kicked in the gut, he'll help you catch your breath" (Psalm 34:18, *The Message*).

"Know I am with you, and I will watch over you no matter where you go" (Genesis 28:15, VOICE).

"When trials come your way—as inevitably they will—do not run away . . . And don't make the mistake in the midst of your trial of not recognizing the goodness of God in allowing the trial."

—Kay Arthur

"You may readily judge whether you are a child of God or a hypocrite by seeing in what direction your soul turns in seasons of severe trial. The hypocrite flies to the world and finds a sort of comfort there, but the child of God runs to his Father and expects consolation only from the Lord's hand!"

—Charles H. Spurgeon

"Having answers is not essential to living. What is essential is the sense of God's presence during dark seasons of questioning."

—Calvin Miller

"If we will only surrender ourselves utterly to the Lord, and will trust Him perfectly, we shall find our souls 'mounting up with wings as eagles' to the 'heavenly places' in Christ Jesus, where earthly annoyances or sorrows have no power to disturb us."

—Hannah Whitall Smith

Greetings, God

Here's what I'm thinking:

Here's what I'm feeling:

Here's how we can do this together:

The fundamental fact of existence is that this trust in God, this faith, is the firm foundation under everything that makes life worth living. It's our handle on what we can't see"

—Hebrews 11:1, *The Message*

CHAPTER 3

A Prayer of Perspective

O Lord, Your ways breathe life. Your discipline gifts wholeness, balance, and peace of heart. You restore. You give me a new lease on life.

I can see this bitter pill is not killing me, but healing me. My trials test me—and that's a good thing. For You, God, deliver me from death. You erase all records of my reckless stupidity and defiant disobedience. You throw me a lifeline and pull me from this black hole of misery.

The dead cannot sing of Your deliverance. Corpses cannot hope or find You faithful. Hymns of praise do not rise from the dark realm.

But ah, the living! Now that's a different story, that's *my* story! For I am alive and leaning into You today. I join the choir of grateful voices belting out accolades of appreciation to You. And our song of thanks will echo throughout time, for all generations, forever and ever. Amen (Isaiah 38:16-19, The Haff Version).

Years ago, a philosophy professor at a prestigious university gave his students one question for the final exam. Placing a chair on top of his desk, he challenged the class by saying, "Using what you have learned this semester, prove to me that this chair does not exist."

Most of the students wrote feverishly for the entire hour. They cited heady theories and well-known philosophers. They used complex logic and debate techniques to "prove" the chair out of existence.

One student, though, wrote his name and scribbled a two-word answer. As it turned out, he was the only student who received an "A" on the final.

All he wrote was this: "What chair?"

As it turned out, only one student chose to see what others failed to see—an empty desk. Similarly, Christians view the world through a different lens. By faith we see what others don't see. Equally important, we don't see what others see. Scripture says, "The fundamental fact of existence is that this trust in God, this faith, is the firm foundation under everything that makes life worth living. It's our handle on what we can't see" (Hebrews 11:1, *The Message*).

So, what is it that you can't see? Perhaps you can't see yourself as a great leader for God. Or you can't see yourself as being forgiven after your titanic blunder. Or you can't see God making good on His promises.

If you struggle to view life through the lens of faith, relax.

You're in good company. Moses stuttered excuses, but God made him into a great leader anyway. Peter messed up in spectacular style, but Jesus accepted him back. And Sarah laughed in God's face when He promised her a child, only to laugh more when she delivered at the advanced age of ninety.

Like the saints of old, we too can enter into an adventure with God and live by faith.

Faith means seeing God in all circumstances. It means trusting in Him enough to do what He prompts you to do—regardless of the consequences. It is the inner conviction that God's way is the best way.

And in the end, only those who live with this faith perspective will pass the final exam.

"O Lord, by these *things men* live;
And in all these *things is* the life of my spirit;
So You will restore me and make me live.
Indeed *it was* for *my own* peace
That I had great bitterness;
But You have lovingly *delivered* my soul from the pit of
    corruption,
For You have cast all my sins behind Your back.
For Sheol cannot thank You,
Death cannot praise You;

Those who go down to the pit cannot hope for Your
   truth.
The living, the living man, he shall praise You,
As I *do* this day;
The father shall make known Your truth to the chil-
   dren" (Isaiah 38:16–19, NKJV).

"We are confident that God is able to orchestrate
everything to work toward something good *and beau-
tiful* when we love Him and accept His invitation to
live according to His plan" (Romans 8:28, VOICE).

"For all of God's promises have been fulfilled in
Christ with a resounding 'Yes!' And through Christ,
our 'Amen' (which means 'Yes') ascends to God for
his glory" (2 Corinthians 1:20, NLT).

"We can complain because rose bushes have thorns, or rejoice because thorns have roses."
—Jean-Baptiste Alphonse Karr, translated from French

"It is a choice to see things differently. When choosing to be grateful you are focusing on all the things that are good or right in your life as opposed to the things that are not. Focus acts like a magnet; you attract those things on which you focus. By focusing on the things you are grateful for, you give those aspects of your life more power. Your world begins to feel more full and alive."
—Ian Sauber

"We need to cultivate a spirit of cheerfulness . . . Let us ever look on the bright side of life, and be hopeful, full of love and good works, rejoicing in the Lord always."
—Ellen G. White

"Cultivate the thankful spirit! It will be to you a perpetual feast."
—John R. MacDuff

Greetings. God

Here's what I'm thinking:

Here's what I'm feeling:

Here's how we can do this together:

CHAPTER 4

A Memory Memo

To: You
From: God
Date: Today
Subject: A Tender Reminder

"Are you scared? Don't be. I'm right here with you.

"Feeling discouraged? Remember, I've not let you out of My care since the moment I created you in your mother's womb.

"I will help you. And hold you. And together, we'll tackle one day at a time.

"I got a firm grip on you. Do you remember when you'd lead your kid across a busy street? No way you'd let loose of that little hand to wander into harm's way. Rest assured, you are in My right hand and I'm not about to let you go it alone.

"Believe Me: This enemy that taunts you will not get

the last word. Not a trace of this invader will remain, not even a memory.

"I am your Daddy who loves you to the moon (that I made!) and back. So I'm sending this short memo to remind you: Don't panic. We got this. Never forget, I will get you through it" (Isaiah 41:10-13, The Haff Version).

It was 12:35 p.m. on September 12, 2001—twenty-seven hours after the terrorist attack on the Twin Towers. Amazingly, Genelle Guzman McMillan was still alive. Although the thirty-year-old Port Authority clerk had fallen from the sixty-fourth floor of the North Tower, she had survived. Barely. Now she was in desperate need of rescue from the ten stories of smoking rubble that entombed her.

Her head was pressed between chunks of concrete while her legs were sandwiched by the twisted fragments of a stairway. From the smoldering debris, she reached into the darkness. But there was no one to hold her hand.

"I kept my hand out there," Genelle said later.

Then she prayed to the God she'd rejected earlier in her life. "Show me a sign. Show me a miracle. Show me that you're out there. Show me that you are listening to me."

Soon, someone grabbed her hand. A gentle voice introduced

himself as Paul. Although Genelle tried to open her eyes, she could not. Paul reassured her that she would survive.

According to a newspaper report, she grabbed his hand. She remembers he was not wearing gloves—unlike the firefighter who found her. "He was holding my hand for a long time," she recalls. "And then other workers came and pulled me out." Rescuers took her to a hospital where she spent the next five weeks. She would never hear from Paul again. "An angel," Genelle says of him.

Genelle Guzman McMillan was the last person pulled alive from the wreckage.[1] But she is not the last person to experience being held by God when hope wanes and the world weighs heavy.

When you are spent and your faith falters, remember this: God holds your hand and whispers, "I will never, *never* forsake you."

So don't be afraid. I am here, with you;
    don't be dismayed, for I am your God.
I will strengthen you, help you.
    I am here with My right hand to make right and to
       hold you up.
Look, everyone who hated you *and sought to do you*
       wrong

will be embarrassed and confused.
Whoever challenged you *with hot-headed bluster*
　　will become as if they never were, and
　　　　nevermore will be.
You may go looking for them, but you won't find them;
　　because those who tried to fight with you will
　　　　become as if they never were.
After all, it is I, the Eternal One your God,
　　who has hold of your right hand,
Who whispers *in your ear*, "Don't be afraid. I will help
　　you" (Isaiah 41:10–13, VOICE).

"He remembers his covenant forever, the promise
he made, for a thousand generations" (1 Chronicles
16:15, NIV).

"Remember the things I have done in the past. For I
alone am God! I am God, and there is none like me"
(Isaiah 46:9, NLT).

"Hope begins in the dark, the stubborn hope that if you just show up and try to do the right thing, the dawn will come. You wait and watch and work: you don't give up."

—Anne Lamott

"Remember Whose you are and Whom you serve. Provoke yourself by recollection, and your affection for God will increase tenfold; your imagination will not be starved any longer, but will be quick and enthusiastic, and your hope will be inexpressibly bright."

—Oswald Chambers

"Jesus gives us hope because He keeps us company, has a vision and knows the way we should go."

—Max Lucado

---

1. Adapted from Mike Kelly, "It Was Heaven on a Hellish Day, Last Survivor Says of Her Angel," *Bergen County* (N.J.) *Record*, September 11, 2003, as seen at Free Republic, http://freerepublic.com/focus/f-news/980933/posts.

Greetings, God

Here's what I'm thinking:

Here's what I'm feeling:

Here's how we can do this together:

CHAPTER 5

When You're Between a Rock and a Hard Place

Do not be afraid. I made you. I brought you into this world. And I got your back.

When you're in a typhoon of trouble, I'm right there with you. When rivers of distress are raging over you, I am your life preserver.

When the inferno of anguish scorches your soul, press on! I am your fire extinguisher. You will not be consumed in the flames.

I promise.

Remember this: I am your personal friend. I got nations at My disposal and I'll gladly cash 'em all in to come to your rescue. That's how much I love you!

You are not forgotten. You are not forsaken. You are loved" (Isaiah 43:1-3, The Haff Version).

Heeeeelp! Heeeeelp!" My wife, Cherié, and I franti-
cally thrashed in hopes of catching a lifeguard's—or
anyone's—attention. But the likelihood of not drowning
seemed about the same as trying to float a wrecking ball.

Although we considered ourselves strong and steady swim-
mers (both certified lifeguards), the riptides in Mazatlán, Mexico
proved a superior match. While bodysurfing, the current caught
us unaware and sucked us into the open sea. Now we were
paralyzed by panic, certain that we were facing the end.

"Don't panic," Cherié gasped. "Just float."

"No!" I said. "Floating will just take us farther out. Swim
with all you got."

We flailed about like spiders swimming up a gushing
fire-hydrant hose. Exhausted, we shared what we thought
to be our final prayer and good-byes.

In that moment of hopelessness, I felt something under
my feet. First, I thought it was a shark. Then I realized it was
a rock. Shaking, crying, and hyperventilating all at the same
time, we clutched on to each other as we tried to balance
ourselves against the angry waves. "Okay," I coached, "let's
wait here until we get enough strength to make it in."

We prayed. We rested. We formulated a strategy. "We're
never going to make it if we go straight toward the shore,"
Cherié said. "The current is too strong. We need to swim
almost parallel to the beach and slowly angle in that direction."

Twenty minutes later we pushed away with another prayer.

"God, please, get us home."

Battling fierce waves and unrelenting currents, we inched toward the goal. With dogged focus and reluctant muscles, we pressed on. At last we triumphantly collapsed in one another's arms on shore.

Clutching each other, we had an impromptu and tearful debriefing. "Thank God we're alive. I have never been so terrified in all my life. Thank God."

Now, thirty years later, the memory still triggers trembling fingers as I type. Had it not been for that rock there's no doubt in my mind that we would have been statistics. When you know you're about to drown there is nothing better than to find firm footing on a solid foundation.

That is helpful to remember when you're overwhelmed by the inevitable storms of life. When it feels most helpless, remember that you can trust God. He may not do what you want, but He will always do what is right, and ultimately what is best. In that assurance you can feel peace over panic. You can make decisions in full confidence that God knows what He's doing. So trust in His strength rather than your own and He will take care of you.

But now, thus says the LORD, who created you,
    O Jacob,
And He who formed you, O Israel:
"Fear not, for I have redeemed you;
I have called *you* by your name;
You *are* Mine.
When you pass through the waters, I *will be* with you;
And through the rivers, they shall not overflow you.
When you walk through the fire, you shall not be
    burned,
Nor shall the flame scorch you.
For I *am* the LORD your God,
The Holy One of Israel, your Savior (Isaiah 43:1–3,
    NKJV).

" 'LORD, help!' they cried in their trouble,
    and he saved them from their distress.
He calmed the storm to a whisper
    and stilled the waves.
What a blessing was that stillness
    as he brought them safely into harbor!
Let them praise the LORD for his great love
    and for the wonderful things he has done for them"
      (Psalm 107:28–31, NLT).

"GOD is good,
a hiding place in tough times.
He recognizes and welcomes
anyone looking for help,
No matter how desperate the trouble" (Nahum
1:7–10, *The Message*).

"The LORD is my rock, my fortress, and my savior;
My God is my rock, in whom I find protection.
He is my shield, the power that saves me,
and my place of safety" (Psalm 18:2 NLT).

"Storms make trees take deeper roots."

—Dolly Parton

"Hope is like an anchor. Our hope in Christ stabilizes us in the storms of life, but unlike an anchor, it does not hold us back."

—Charles R. Swindoll

"There is only one secure foundation: a genuine, saving relationship with Jesus Christ, which will carry us through any and all turmoil. No matter what storms are raging all around, you'll stand firm if you stand on His love."

—Charles Stanley

God "sometimes lets us hit rock-bottom so we can discover that He is the Rock at the bottom."

—Tony Evans

Greetings, God

Here's what I'm thinking:

Here's what I'm feeling:

Here's how we can do this together:

Therefore, since we have been made right in God's sight by faith, we have peace with God because of what Jesus Christ our Lord has done for us.

—Romans 5:1, NLT

CHAPTER 6

I Do Declare!

I declare under penalty of perjury per the law of God:

That, in Jesus, I am set right with God. My forever is sure. And I have all-access to God's peace, grace, and hope.

That, even in seasons of suffering, I will proclaim His praise. For I know that suffering grows grit in me that will get me through any grief. The grief forges character. And out of character comes my vision to see that God will *always* do good by me. ALWAYS!

That, my hope in God is steadfast. He fills my deepest need. He floods my heart with His Holy Spirit. And my life overflows in His love.

This is my witness. So help me God" (Romans 5:1–5, The Haff Version).

On his thirty-ninth birthday, poet Christian Wiman was diagnosed with an incurable form of blood cancer. He described his disease in this way: "I have had bones die and bowels fail; joints lock in my face and arms and legs, so that I could not eat, could not walk . . . I have passed through pain I could never have imagined, pain that seemed to incinerate all my thoughts of God and to leave me sitting there in the ashes, alone."

Ironically, this horrific disease sparked his journey back to God. It wasn't a particular doctrine that drew him back to faith, but Wiman found a friend in the suffering Messiah.

I am a Christian because of that moment on the cross when Jesus, drinking the very dregs of human bitterness, cries out, "My God, my God, why has thou forsaken me." . . . The point is that God is with us, not beyond us, in suffering. I am a Christian because I understand that moment of Christ's passion to have meaning in my own life, and what it means is that the absolute solitary and singular nature of extreme human pain is an illusion. . . . Christ's suffering shatters the iron walls around individual human suffering.[1]

In the face of raw, isolating pain we don't really want answers. We want a person. At such times there is simply no substitute for the presence of Christ.

Therefore, since we have been made right in God's sight by faith, we have peace with God because of what Jesus Christ our Lord has done for us. Because of our faith, Christ has brought us into this place of undeserved privilege where we now stand, and we confidently and joyfully look forward to sharing God's glory.

We can rejoice, too, when we run into problems and trials, for we know that they help us develop endurance. And endurance develops strength of character, and character strengthens our confident hope of salvation. And this hope will not lead to disappointment. For we know how dearly God loves us, because he has given us the Holy Spirit to fill our hearts with his love (Romans 5:1–5, NLT).

"Therefore, since Christ suffered in his body, arm yourselves also with the same attitude, because whoever suffers in the body is done with sin" (1 Peter 4:1, NIV).

"I have told you these things so that you will be *whole and* at peace. In this world, you will be plagued with times of trouble, but you need not fear; I have triumphed over this corrupt world order" (John 16:33, VOICE).

"A story is being written, with an ending only faintly glimpsed by us. We face the choice of trusting the Author along the way or striking out alone. Always, we have the choice."
—Philip Yancey

"I can say with complete truthfulness that everything I have learned in my seventy-five years in this world, everything that has truly enhanced and enlightened my experience, has been through affliction and not through happiness."
—Malcolm Muggeridge

"Those who are willing to suffer for Christ will experience more joy in suffering than in the fact that Christ has suffered for them, thus showing that He loved them. Those who win heaven will put forth their noblest efforts, and will labor with all long-suffering, that they may reap the fruit of toil."
—Ellen G. White

---

1. Drew Dyck, *Yawning at Tigers: You Can't Tame God, So Stop Trying* (Nashville, TN: Nelson Books, 2014), 150, 151.

Greetings, God

Here's what I'm thinking:

Here's what I'm feeling:

Here's how we can do this together:

CHAPTER 7

Pay Hope Forward

"Praise God, the Father of our leader, Jesus Christ, the Anointed One. He is compassionate. He brings comfort. He heals us. Our struggles are no match for His strength.

He consoles us in our pain. In every setback, He is there. Problems persist, but His presence prevails.

God carries us through the calamities so that we can pay hope forward to others in crisis. Just as God was there for us, so we can show up for others" (2 Corinthians 1:3, 4, The Haff Version).

Kate Bowler is an associate professor at Duke Divinity School. In her memoir, *Everything Happens for A Reason: And Other Lies I've Loved*, Bowler tells of her fight with stage 4 cancer. In an interview on NPR's *Fresh Air*, she shared the story of her struggles.

She said that of course she wanted a long life with her husband and young son. But in her pain, she discovered "a gift"—she realized how fragile life is for everyone. And that insight connected her with the pain of other people. Bowler explains:

It's like you notice the tired mom in the grocery store who's just like struggling to get the thing off the top shelf while her kid screams, and you notice how very tired that person looks at the bus stop. And then, of course, all the people in the cancer clinic around me. That felt like I was cracked open, and I could see everything really clearly for the first time. And the other bit was not feeling nearly as angry as I thought I would. And, I mean, granted—like I have been pretty angry at times. But it was mostly that I felt God's presence. And it was less like, here are some important spiritual truths I know intellectually about God . . . It was instead more like the way you'd feel a friend or like someone holding you. I just didn't feel quite as scared. I just felt loved [by God].[1]

"All praise to God, the Father of our Lord Jesus Christ. God is our merciful Father and the source of all comfort. He comforts us in all our troubles so that we can comfort others. When they are troubled, we will be able to give them the same comfort God has given us" (2 Corinthians 1:3, 4, NLT).

"Jesus sent his twelve harvest hands out with this charge:

"Don't begin by traveling to some far-off place to convert unbelievers. And don't try to be dramatic by tackling some public enemy. Go to the lost, confused people right here in the neighborhood. Tell them that the kingdom is here. Bring health to the sick. Raise the dead. Touch the untouchables. Kick out the demons. You have been treated generously, so live generously" (Matthew 10:5–8, *The Message*).

"Then he said, 'Do you understand what I have done to you? You address me as 'Teacher' and 'Master,' and rightly so. That is what I am. So if I, the Master and Teacher, washed your feet, you must now wash each other's feet. I've laid down a pattern for you. What I've done, you do. I'm only pointing out the obvious. A servant is not ranked above his master; an employee doesn't give orders to the employer. If you understand what I'm telling you, act like it—and live a blessed life" (John 13:15–17, *The Message*).

"If you want to lift yourself up, lift up someone else."
—Booker T. Washington

"Small acts, when multiplied by millions of people, can transform the world."
—Howard Zinn

"Only a life lived for others is a life worthwhile."
—Albert Einstein

"The purpose of life is not to be happy. It is to be useful, to be honorable, to be compassionate, to have it make some difference that you have lived and lived well."
—Ralph Waldo Emerson

"A candle loses nothing by lighting another candle."
—James Keller

1. Terry Gross, "A Stage4 Cancer patient Shares the Pain and Clarity of Living 'Scan-to-Scan,' " NPR *Fresh Air*, February 12, 2018, https://www.npr.org/programs/fresh-air/2018/02/12/585080743/fresh-air-for-feb-12-2018-living-with-incurable-stage-4-cancer.

Greetings, God

Here's what I'm thinking:

Here's what I'm feeling:

Here's how we can do this together:

CHAPTER 8

Seeing the Unseen

Dear Disease,

You will not defeat me. I will not despair. Nor will I be discouraged.

Yes, you are battering my physical body. From all outward appearances, it seems you've got the upper hand. But you cannot touch my spirit within. Every day, God renews me from the inside and you are powerless to trespass upon His domain.

Everything you're throwing at me these days cowers in comparison to what I've got coming for eternity.

So, I am serving you notice. My focus is fixed—not on what is seen, but on the unseen. Docs see scans and prescriptions and probabilities. I see everlasting hope and healing and heaven.

Your days are numbered, mine are not. Your terror is temporary. My faith is forever.

In holy defiance, God's beloved kid (2 Corinthians 4:16–18, The Haff Version).

Carolyn Arends recounts a disturbing yet impactful story she heard as a kid in church. Missionaries on furlough told of an enormous snake that slithered into their kitchen. Terrified, they screamed for a local to come to their aid. A machete-wielding native appeared and decapitated the invader with one swift chop. Disaster averted . . . but there was a catch. It would be a while before the snake died.

Arends explains:

A snake's neurology and blood flow are such that it can take considerable time for it to stop moving even after decapitation. For the next several hours, the missionaries were forced to wait outside while the snake thrashed about, smashing furniture and flailing against walls and windows, wreaking havoc until its body finally understood that it no longer had a head.

Sweating in the heat, they had felt frustrated and a little sickened but also grateful that the snake's rampage wouldn't last forever.[1]

In the Garden of Eden, a snake disrupted the plan of our kind God for us to live in a perfect world free of tears, heartbreak, and death. "God told the serpent: 'Because you've done this, you're cursed, . . . I'm declaring war between you and the Woman, between your offspring and hers. He'll wound your head, you'll wound his heel' " (Genesis 3:14, 15, *The Message*).

Yes, the serpent will cause messy mayhem in this world; or, as Scripture puts it, he will wound the Savior's heel, but at a cost, his own head would be crushed.

We see the serpent's thrashing, don't we? Violence thrives. Evil dominates minds. Disease destroys bodies. But Jesus has smashed the serpent's head and will ultimately restore order, once and for all. Evil will not have the last word. The snake will stop. And this world will be set right.

So we have no reason to despair. Despite the fact that our outer humanity is falling apart and decaying, our inner humanity is breathing in new life every day. You see, the short-lived pains of this life are creating for us an eternal glory that does not compare to anything we know here. So we do not set our sights on the things we can see *with our eyes*. All of that is fleeting; *it will eventually fade away*. Instead, we focus on the things we cannot see, which live on and on (2 Corinthians 4:16–18, VOICE).

"Because God's children are human beings—made of flesh and blood—the Son also became flesh and blood. For only as a human being could he die, and only by dying could he break the power of the devil, who had the power of death. Only in this way could he set free all who have lived their lives as slaves to the fear of dying" (Hebrews 2:14, 15, NLT).

"Together they will go to war against the Lamb, but the Lamb will defeat them because he is Lord of all lords and King of all kings. And his called and chosen and faithful ones will be with him" (Revelation 17:14, NLT).

"The last enemy to be destroyed is death" (1 Corinthians 15:26, NIV).

"The eternal Son of God had to become man—because it was the offspring of the woman who was to crush the serpent's head."

—John Piper

"There's nothing more calming in difficult moments than knowing there's someone fighting with you."

—Mother Teresa

"The best we can hope for in this life is a knothole peek at the shining realities ahead. Yet a glimpse is enough. It's enough to convince our hearts that whatever sufferings and sorrows currently assail us aren't worthy of comparison to that which waits over the horizon."

—Joni Eareckson Tada

1. Carolyn Arends, "Satan's a Goner: A Lesson From a Headless Snake," *Christianity Today*, February 2011, https://www.christianity today.com/ct/2011/february/satansagoner.html.

Greetings, God

Here's what I'm thinking:

Here's what I'm feeling:

Here's how we can do this together:

CHAPTER 9

Prescription for Peace

FOR: You

AILMENT: Anxiety

FROM: The Great Physician

DATE: Today

"Don't fret.

Just ask.

Turn your worrying into praying.

Tell Me what you need. And reflect on what you have.

Side effects include:

Peace beyond understanding.

Calm thoughts.

A quiet heart.

Your soul at rest" (Philippians 4:6, 7, The Haff Version).

When Mark Twain was a young man, he worked as an editor and publisher of a growing newspaper in a small Missouri town. One day he received a letter from one of his subscribers. The subscriber said that he had found a spider in that morning's edition of his paper. He wanted to know if this was an omen of good luck or bad luck.

Twain, a hustling salesman as well as an editor, wrote to his customer: "Dear Sir: Finding the spider in your newspaper yesterday morning was neither good luck nor bad luck for you. The spider was merely looking over our paper to see which of the town's merchants is not advertising. He will then go to that store, spin his web across the door, and live a life of undisturbed peace."

Beyond the meaning of Mark Twain's sales pitch, the idea of a life of undisturbed peace sounds inviting, doesn't it? Who isn't looking for "a life of undisturbed peace?" Peace when the diagnosis looks grim. Peace when the marriage is frayed. Peace in pain. The fact is that this kind of peace is only found in God. As C. S. Lewis put it, "God cannot give us . . . peace apart from Himself, because it is not there. There is no such thing."

"Be anxious for nothing, but in everything by prayer and supplication, with thanksgiving, let your requests be made known to God; and the peace of God, which surpasses all understanding, will guard your hearts and minds through Christ Jesus" (Philippians 4:6, 7, NKJV).

"I will see to it that you have peace in your land. You will be able to go to bed at night without a worry on your mind" (Leviticus 26:6, VOICE).

"*Tonight* I will sleep securely on a bed of peace because I trust You, You alone, O Eternal One, will keep me safe" (Psalm 4:8, VOICE).

The LORD gives his people strength. The LORD blesses them with peace (Psalm 29:11, NLT).

You will keep in perfect peace those whose minds are steadfast, because they trust in you (Isaiah 26:3, NIV).

May the Lord make His face shine upon you, and be kind to you. May the Lord show favor toward you, and give you peace (Numbers 6:25, 26, NLV).

"A great many people are trying to make peace. But that has already been done. God has not left it for us to do; all that we have to do is to enter into it."

—Dwight L. Moody

"Unless you wholly give yourself up to the Life of our Lord Jesus Christ, and resign your will wholly to Him, and desire nothing without Him, you shall never come to such a rest as no Creature can disturb . . . You shall find that in your own power, and without such a total surrender to God, and to the Life of God, you can never arrive at such a rest as this, or the true quiet of the soul, wherein no Creature can molest you, or so much as touch you."

—Jacob Boehme

"Courage for the great sorrows of life, and patience for the small ones. And then when you have laboriously accomplished your daily task, go to sleep in peace. God is awake."

—Victor Hugo

"When we put our problems in God's hands, He puts His peace in our hearts."

—Anonymous

"Never be in a hurry; do everything quietly and in a calm spirit. Do not lose your inner peace for anything whatsoever, even if your whole world seems upset."

—Saint Francis de Sales

Greetings, God

Here's what I'm thinking:

Here's what I'm feeling:

Here's how we can do this together:

CHAPTER 10

The Caregiver's Psalm

The Lord is my Caregiver. He'll see to it that I've got everything I truly need. He gives me a good, restful night of sleep.

He captains my rickety raft through whitewater and guides me into the tranquil harbor.

He builds my spiritual muscles.

He leads me on the best path to bring glory to His name.

Even if the diagnosis is dark:

"The lump is malignant."

"Full recovery is unlikely."

"There's nothing more that we can do."

I will not be afraid, because my Friend is with me.

Your closeness comforts me. Sure, there are dangers that I fear, but I can always count on You for my next meal, my daily bread, a cup of cool water.

You drench me with Your blessings.

Laughter.

Waterfalls.

Friends.

Sunsets.

Conversations.

Music.

Hugs.

Even in the driest season, you fill my barrel to overflowing.

Your goodness and love will blanket me all my life, and I will live in the house of the Lord forever.

Amen (Psalm 23, The Haff Version).

Someone suggested the phrase in Psalm 23:6 that states, "Surely goodness and mercy shall follow me all the days of my life" might refer to angels—one named "Goodness" and the other named "Mercy."

On the blog Christian Motivations, the story is posted of an elderly man and his wife stranded by their truck, waving for help. A Good Samaritan stopped and asked what was wrong.

The elderly man said that he was a pastor, and he and his wife were heading to the town up the road but feared they might run out of gas. "Could you give me a ride to the nearest gas station?"

"Sure," the good Samaritan said, "but since you're not out of gas yet, why don't you just head towards the next gas station? I will follow behind you, and if you do run out of gas, I will take you to get gas from there—but at least you'll be closer."

For the next twenty miles, the pastor relaxed as they cruised to the next station. His truck never did run out of gas. As he was filling up, he thanked the good Samaritan again. "Just knowing you were behind us," he said, "in case we did run out of gas, allowed my wife and I to drive without worry."[1]

You can enjoy the same assurance. Just knowing that God will never forsake you allows you to press forward without worry or fear. The angels, whether they are called "Goodness" and "Mercy" or by some other names, will always be squarely in your rear-view mirror.

The LORD is my shepherd; I shall not want.

He maketh me to lie down in green pastures: he leadeth me beside the still waters.

He restoreth my soul: he leadeth me in the paths of righteousness for his name's sake.

Yea, though I walk through the valley of the shadow of death, I will fear no evil: for thou art with me; thy rod and thy staff they comfort me.

Thou preparest a table before me in the presence of mine enemies: thou anointest my head with oil; my cup runneth over.

Surely goodness and mercy shall follow me all the days of my life: and I will dwell in the house of the Lord forever (Psalm 23).

"Don't be obsessed with getting more material things. Be relaxed with what you have. Since God assured us, 'I'll never let you down, never walk off and leave you,' we can boldly quote, 'God is there, ready to help; I'm fearless no matter what. Who or what can get to me?' " (Hebrews 13:5, 6, *The Message*).

"Know this: my God will also fill every need you have according to His glorious riches in Jesus the Anointed, *our Liberating King"* (Philippians 4:19, VOICE).

"We have an enemy inside of us who tries to convince us that there is something out there that is better than what God wants for us, but that's not true. Every day I remind myself that what God is providing is always the best thing for me."
—Lauryn Hill

"We can be certain that God will give us the strength and resources we need to live through any situation in life that He ordains. The will of God will never take us where the grace of God cannot sustain us."

—Billy Graham

"A God wise enough to create me and the world I live in is wise enough to watch out for me."

—Philip Yancey

"Your job is to abide in my pasture
Eating sweet grass and drinking pure water,
And sharing both with others—
That is a lamb's business."

—Jessica Coupé

"I have all things and abound; not because I have a good store of money in the bank, not because I have skill and wit with which to win my bread, but because the 'Lord is my shepherd.' "

—Charles H. Spurgeon

---

1. Andre Schoonbee, "Goodness and Mercy," *Christian Motivations*, March 12, 2013, http://christianmotivations.weebly.com/christian-motivations-blog/archives/03-2013/18.

Greetings, God

Here's what I'm thinking:

Here's what I'm feeling:

Here's how we can do this together:

CHAPTER 11

An Upward View When You Are Down

Misery is my middle name. I am desperate. Overwhelmed. Drunk in dismay.

The enemy has moved into my neighborhood. He taunts me. And mocks my family.

But I'm not giving up. My focus is fixed on my Father in heaven. My hope is in Him. He will hear me. He will save me.

I am putting the enemy on notice: Stop crowing over me. I am down, but I am not out. Darkness swallows me, but it cannot extinguish the light of God in me.

I'm a flawed sinner. I get that. And I deserve the discipline of God. Fair enough. But I know it is a temporary matter and, in the end, God has my back. He will shine his light on me, and I will revel in his dazzling brightness.

The scoffers who taunt me, asking "Where's your oh-so-wonderful God now?" will get their due. At last, I will see their collapse as they get trampled on like mud in the street. That will be a great day of rebuilding, healing and complete restoration! (Micah 7:1, 6–11, The Haff Version).

During the Vietnam War, Vice Admiral James Stockdale was ruthlessly beaten for nearly eight years at the infamous "Hanoi Hilton." As the highest-ranking prisoner of war, he led a resistance movement and established a code of conduct that all prisoners pledged to uphold—including the proper response to torture. Eventually, he and nearly a dozen of the other prisoners landed in a cell dubbed "Alcatraz"—a three-foot-by-nine-foot chamber with a light bulb that burned nonstop. Every night they were locked in leg irons.

In spite of the horrific circumstances, however, Stockdale's unwavering resolve never broke. In February 1973, he was released—his body so mangled he could barely walk.

In his book, *Good to Great*, Jim Collins tells of his conversation with Stockdale. Collins wanted to know how anyone could survive such an ordeal and then move on to lead a productive life.

"I never lost faith in the end of the story," he said, . . . "I never doubted not only that I would get out, but also that I would prevail in the end and turn the experience into the defining event of my life, which, in retrospect, I would not trade." . . .

[Collins then] asked, "Who didn't make it out?". . .

"The optimists . . . they were the ones who said, 'We're going to be out by Christmas.' And Christmas would come, and Christmas would go. Then they'd say, 'We're going to be out by Easter.' And Easter would come, and Easter would go. And then Thanksgiving, and then it would be Christmas again. And they died of a broken heart."[1]

As you endure seasons of suffering, never lose sight of the end of your story. Remember that authentic faith is not some Pollyanna, positive-thinking charade; rather, it is the paradoxical discipline that combines harsh reality and real hope. It embraces the twin truths of present challenge and ultimate triumph. Real freedom comes to those who can link the appalling present with the promising future, while depending always on our faithful God for final deliverance.

Woe is me! . . . For the son dishonoureth the father, the daughter riseth up against her mother, the daughter in law against her mother in law; a man's enemies are the men of his own house…. Therefore I will look unto the LORD; I will wait for the God of my salvation: my God will hear me. Rejoice not against me, O mine enemy: when I fall, I shall arise; when I sit in darkness, the LORD shall be a light unto me. I will bear the indignation of the Lord, because I have sinned against him, until he plead my cause, and execute judgment for me: he will bring me forth to the light, and I shall behold his righteousness. Then she that is mine enemy shall see it, and shame shall cover her which said unto me, "Where is the LORD thy God?" mine eyes shall behold her: now shall she be trodden down as the mire of the streets. In the day that thy walls are to be built, in that day shall the decree be far removed (Micah 7:1, 6–11).

"Praise be to the God and Father of our Lord Jesus Christ! In his great mercy he has given us new birth into a living hope through the resurrection of Jesus Christ from the dead, and into an inheritance that can never perish, spoil or fade. This inheritance is kept in heaven for you" (1 Peter 1:3, 4, NIV).

"And so, Lord, where do I put my hope? My only hope is in you" (Psalm 39:7, NLT).

"Everything works out in the end. If it hasn't worked out yet, then it's not the end."

—Anonymous

"Faith don't come in a bushel basket, Missy. It come one step at a time. Decide to trust Him for one little thing today, and before you know it, you find out He's so trustworthy you be putting your whole life in His hands."

—Lynn Austin

"Fear is the glue that keeps you stuck. Faith is the solvent that sets you free."

—Shannon L. Alder

"Pray, and let God worry."

—Martin Luther

"Hope is never wasted. Even if what I hoped for did not come to fruition as I had imagined, as I had hoped. Hope is placing the beautifully vulnerable parts of ourselves, our raw selves, into His hands. I believe hope moves His heart; but hope also moves our hearts into His hands. Hope builds trust."

—Natalie Brenner

---

1. Jim Collins, *Good to Great: Why Some Companies Make the Leap . . . and Others Don't* (New York: HarperBusiness, 2001), 85.

Greetings, God

Here's what I'm thinking:

Here's what I'm feeling:

Here's how we can do this together:

CHAPTER 12

Post-op Instruction Sheet

1. **Follow your Physician's orders.** You may think you know what's best moving forward but swallow your pride and obey the Doctor's orders. His strong hand is on you. Trust Him in everything. He *will* restore you to full health.

2. **Offload your anxieties.** Since your Doctor knows you personally and cares unconditionally about you, outsource your stress to Him. He is gentle and kind.

3. **Keep a clear head and stay alert.** BEWARE! Many patients relapse. Infection is always a threat. Disease is the enemy—threatening to destroy you like a lion destroys his prey. Do not let down your guard.

4. **Lean into community.** There are patients all over the world who suffer like you. Keep each other close and remind yourselves, the pain is not permanent.

5. **Commit 1 Peter 5:10, 11 to memory.** Carry this promise in your soul (1 Peter 5:6–11, The Haff Version). "It won't be long before this generous God who has great

plans for us in Christ—eternal and glorious plans they are!—will have you put together and on your feet for good. He gets the last word; yes, he does" (verses 10, 11, *The Message*).

At 10:55 A.M. on December 2, 2015, Denise Peraza and Shannon Johnson were sitting next to each other at a luncheon for the San Bernardino County Department of Public Health. They joked about how the large clock on the wall might be broken because time seemed to be moving so slowly.

Moments later, they were huddled together on the floor using a chair as a shield to protect themselves from two people dressed in black and shooting randomly. Johnson wrapped his left arm around Peraza and held her close.

Peraza was shot once in the back and survived. Johnson died.

From the melee, however, emerged a poignant portrait of heroism and self-sacrifice. Peraza would later issue this statement:

"While I cannot recall every single second that played out that morning, I will always remember his left arm wrapped around me, holding me as close as possible next to him behind that chair.

"And amidst all the chaos, I'll always remember him saying these three words, 'I got you.' "[1]

Always remember these three words: "I got you." These are God's three words to you. And not just in time of need, but all the time. He is your loving Father who will never leave you nor forsake you. He says to you, "I got you, I got you, I got you."

So be content with who you are, and don't put on airs. God's strong hand is on you; he'll promote you at the right time. Live carefree before God; he is most careful with you.

Keep a cool head. Stay alert. The Devil is poised to pounce, and would like nothing better than to catch you napping. Keep your guard up. You're not the only ones plunged into these hard times. It's the same with Christians all over the world. So keep a firm grip on the faith. The suffering won't last forever. It won't be long before this generous God who has great plans for us in Christ—eternal and glorious plans they are!—will have you put together and on your feet for good. He gets the last word; yes, he does (1 Peter 5:6–11, *The Message*).

"I will ask the Father to send you another Helper, *the Spirit of truth*, who will remain constantly with you. The world does not recognize the Spirit of truth, because it does not know the Spirit and is unable to receive Him. But you do know the Spirit because He lives with you, and He will dwell in you. I will never abandon you like orphans; I will return to be with you" (John 14:16–18, VOICE).

Then, *oh then*, your light will break out like the *warm,*
    golden rays of a rising sun;
  in an instant, you will be healed.
Your rightness will precede *and protect* you;
  the glory of the Eternal will follow and defend you.
Then when you do call out, *"My God, Where are*
  You?"
The Eternal One will answer, "I am here, *I am here*"
  (Isaiah 58:8, 9, VOICE).

"If the Lord be with us, we have no cause of fear. His eye is upon us, his arm over us, his ear open to our prayer; his grace sufficient, his promise unchangeable."
—John Newton

"We need to cry out to the Lord when we feel the waves of terror or anger crashing around us. He is always within reach, ready to stretch out his hand to steady us."

—Shirley Corder

"Do not fear circumstances. They cannot hurt us, if we hold fast by God and use them as the voices and ministries of His will. Trust Him about everyone and everything, for all times and all needs, earth and heaven, friends and children, the conquest of sin, the growth of holiness, the cross that chafes, the grace that stirs."

—Anthony W. Thorold

"Even in terrible circumstances and calamities, in matters of life and death, if I sense that I am in the shadow of God, I find light, so much light that my vision improves dramatically. I know that holiness is near."

—Kathleen Norris

---

1. Sarah Parvini and Cindy Carcamo, " 'I Got You' Are Man's Last Words to Co-worker as Bullets Fly in San Bernardino Rampage," *Los Angeles Times*, December 6, 2015, https://www.latimes.com/local/lanow /la-me-ln-shannon-johnson-hero-denise-peraza-20151205-story.html.

Greetings, God

Here's what I'm thinking:

Here's what I'm feeling:

Here's how we can do this together:

CHAPTER 13

Let God Be God

Riots. Recession. Anti-Semitism. This world is whacked! Where can I go to escape the madness?

God.

I look to the sky and remember Pan Am flight 103; I look to the sea and remember USS Cole; I look to the land and cry for the Twin Towers. Where to hide?

God.

Money. Sex. Power. Ego. Addiction. I am so weak. Where can I find strength?

God.

He is always present in crisis. So why the restless nights? The fidgeting? The high blood pressure?

God is peace.

Through earthquakes, tsunamis, and storms, I will be fearless. For I know that fountains of joy gush from wherever God is. And God is always right next to me.

God is ever present.

Tyrants manipulate. Dictators destroy. Terrorists reign. But God speaks and governments are gagged. A whisper from his throne room and our house of cards collapses.

God is in charge.

So, stop your manic pacing. Observe the power of God. Marvel in His presence as He guts advancing armies and ends evil empires. Just stop. Be still. You will know that God is still God (Psalm 46, The Haff Version).

O nce there was a man who asked God, "Which do you think is harder, to be man or to be God?"

"Being God is much harder," God said. "I must look after the whole universe with its planets and galaxies. All you must worry about is your family and your job."

"True enough," the man said. "But you have infinite time and infinite power. The hard part is not doing the job but doing it within the limits of human strength and the human life span."

"You don't know what you are talking about. It's much harder to be God."

"How can you say that when you have never been human, and I have never been God?" said the man. "What do you say we change places for just one second, so you can know the feeling of being man and I can know what it feels like to be God? Just one second, that's all, and then we'll change back."

God didn't like the idea, but the man kept begging. Finally, God relented. They swapped places. Man became God and God became human.

As the story goes, once man sat on the divine throne, he refused to give God back His place. Ever since, man has ruled the world and God has been in exile.

A fable? Yes. A false picture? Perhaps not.

Is there an arena in your life where you have dethroned God and perched yourself in His stead? Maybe it's a financial issue in which you find it necessary to rob God of tithes and offerings in order to meet your obligations. Maybe it's a time issue. Oh, you want to carve out quality time each day to commune with God but with the deadlines at work and the demands of your calendar, you haven't a moment for Him. Maybe it's a personal issue. You have an ingrained pattern of sin that numbs you and gives you feelings of futility. By escaping into the shadows of compromise you temporarily find relief from your pain.

No matter the issue, the real question is this: Do you trust God to be God when it comes to money matters? Time management? Finding worth only in Him? So, ask yourself: Will I *really* let God run my life?

God is our refuge and strength, a tested help in times of trouble. And so we need not fear even if the world blows up and the mountains crumble into the sea. Let the oceans roar and foam; let the mountains tremble!

There is a river of joy flowing through the city of our God—the sacred home of the God above all gods. God himself is living in that city; therefore it stands unmoved despite the turmoil everywhere. He will not delay his help. The nations rant and rave in anger—but when God speaks, the earth melts in submission and kingdoms totter into ruin.

The Commander of the armies of heaven is here among us. He, the God of Jacob, has come to rescue us.

Come, see the glorious things that our God does, how he brings ruin upon the world and causes wars to end throughout the earth, breaking and burning every weapon. "Stand silent! Know that I am God! I will be honored by every nation in the world!"

The Commander of the heavenly armies is here among *us!* He, the God of Jacob, has come to rescue *us!* (Psalm 46, TLB).

"Lord, when doubts fill my mind, when my heart is in turmoil, quiet me and give me renewed hope and cheer" (Psalm 94:19, TLB).

"The Eternal owns the world; He exercises His *gentle* rule over all the nations" (Psalm 22:28, VOICE).

"The LORD Almighty has sworn, 'Surely, as I have planned, so it will be, and as I have purposed, so it will happen" (Isaiah 14:24, NIV).

"Never be afraid to trust an unknown future to a known God."

—Corrie Ten Boom

"Don't ask God to guide your steps if you're not willing to move your feet."

—Unknown

"The best remedy for those who are frightened, lonely or unhappy is to go outside, somewhere they can be alone, alone with the sky, nature and God. For then and only then can you feel that everything is as it should be."

—Anne Frank

"To learn strong faith is to endure great trials. I have learned my faith by standing firm amid severe testings."
—George Mueller

"Faith is taking the first step even when you don't see the whole staircase."
—Martin Luther King Jr.

Greetings, God

Here's what I'm thinking:

Here's what I'm feeling:

Here's how we can do this together:

We know how much God loves us because we have felt his love and because we believe him when he tells us that he loves us dearly. God is love, and anyone who lives in love is living with God and God is living in him.

—1 John 4:16, TLB

CHAPTER 14

Good Morning, God!

Better than any cappuccino, oh God, is Your love. Your mercies never stop. Your faithful acts of grace warm me afresh every morning. You are the best part of waking up.

I begin each day with this prayer: "I will wait upon You. My hope is always, only, moment by moment in You."

And You are good. So good. Every single drop of life with You is good.

You quiet my anxious heart as I wait for You to set things right in this world.

You guide me through the tough patches. Trouble is always brewing. I only wish I'd trusted You more when I was younger. It is a good lesson to learn early in life—to hang on to hope through life's trying times.

And now once again, here we are. Alone. Pondering the hard work that You give me to do today. So, I bow before You, certain that I have every reason for hope.

Even as my enemies slap me around, I know that You will not ditch me.

Yes, sorrow is always part of the story, but Your great mercy eclipses all dark things. I know Your heart, oh God, and it is good. You do not delight in the demise of Your children.

I know You are with me through all the percolating problems. I know You are good. So bring on the day! (Lamentations 3:22-33, The Haff Version).

William Frey, a retired Episcopal bishop from Colorado, shared the following story:

When I was a younger man, I volunteered to read to a degree student named John who was blind. One day I asked him, "How did you lose your sight?"

"A chemical explosion," John said, "at the age of thirteen."

"How did that make you feel?" I asked.

"Life was over. I felt helpless. I hated God," John responded. "For the first six months I did nothing to improve my lot in life. I would eat all my meals alone in my room. One day my father entered my room and said, 'John, winter's coming and the storm windows need to be up—that's your job. I want those hung by the time I get back this evening or else!'

"Then he turned, walked out of the room and slammed the door. I got so angry. I thought *Who does he think I am? I'm blind!* I was so angry I decided to do it. I felt my way to the garage, found the windows, located the necessary tools, found the ladder, all the while muttering under my breath, 'I'll show them. I'll fall, then they'll have a blind and paralyzed son!' "

John continued, "I got the windows up. I found out later that never at any moment was my father more than four or five feet away from my side."[1]

The father was not about to abandon his boy. Your heavenly Father feels the same way

The father was not about to abandon his boy. Your heavenly Father feels the same way about you. Remember this text: "God is keeping careful watch over us" (1 Peter 1:5, *The Message*). In the struggle, your Father is ever present.

Yet there is one ray of hope: his compassion never ends. It is only the Lord's mercies that have kept us from complete destruction. Great is his faithfulness; his loving-kindness begins afresh each day. My soul claims the Lord as my inheritance; therefore I will hope in him. The Lord is wonderfully good to those who wait for him, to those who seek for him. It is good both to hope and wait quietly for the salvation of the Lord.

It is good for a young man to be under discipline, for it causes him to sit apart in silence beneath the Lord's demands, to lie face downward in the dust; then at last there is hope for him. Let him turn the other cheek to those who strike him and accept their awful insults, for the Lord will not abandon him forever. Although God gives him grief, yet he will show compassion too, according to the greatness of his loving-kindness. For he does not enjoy afflicting men and causing sorrow (Lamentations 3:21–33, TLB).

"And I heard a loud voice from the throne saying, 'Look! God's dwelling place is now among the people, and he will dwell with them. They will be his people, and God himself will be with them and be their God'" (Revelation 21:3, NIV).

"We know how much God loves us because we have felt his love and because we believe him when he tells us that he loves us dearly. God is love, and anyone who lives in love is living with God and God is living in him" (1 John 4:16, TLB).

"The Lord can leave us wanting relative to certain things (sometimes judged indispensable in the eyes of the world), but He never leaves us deprived of what is essential: His presence, His peace and all that is necessary for the complete fulfillment of our lives, according to His plans for us."

—Jacques Philippe

"Do I believe that God is right here, ready to be my comfort in every situation?"

—Erin M. Straza

"Ask God to increase your faith, and then begin living a life that reflects absolute trust in Him."

—Henry T. Blackaby

"Faith is a reasoning trust, a trust which reckons thoughtfully and confidently upon the trustworthiness of God."

—John R. Stott

"The way of Jesus cannot be imposed or mapped—it requires an active participation in following Jesus as he leads us through sometimes strange and unfamiliar territory, in circumstances that become clear only in the hesitations and questionings, in the pauses and reflections where we engage in prayerful conversation with one another and with Him."

—Eugene H. Peterson

1. William Frey, "When Words Come to an End," Beeson Divinity School, July 2003, quoted in "God Is an Arm's-Length Away," PreachingToday, accessed June 19, 2023, https://www.preachingtoday.com /illustrations/2004/january/14778.html.

Greetings, God

Here's what I'm thinking:

Here's what I'm feeling:

Here's how we can do this together:

Let us hold firmly to the hope that we have confessed, because we can trust God to do what he promised.

—Hebrews 10:23, NCV

CHAPTER 15

Promises, Promises

"Though the mountains be shaken and the hills be removed,

"Though thy car crumpleth into the pole,

"Though crooks deleteth thine Capital One account,

"Though the tumor groweth,

"Though the pounds counteth up and the scale mocketh thine diet,

"Though the demons of depression assail thee,

"Though thy mishap goeth viral,

"My unfailing love for you will not be shaken nor My covenant of peace be removed," saith the LORD, who has compassion on thee (Isaiah 54:10, The Haff Version).

I t wasn't that Lance didn't believe in God. He did—so long as God behaved like God. That meant God needed to be a celestial Santa Claus and hand out heaps of health and happiness.

For a while, Lance was a big believer. He aced his classes without studying ("I just prayed, and EUREKA!, God gave me wisdom," he'd say), got a new Mustang convertible for Christmas ("Dad's dot-com company went public"), and his chiseled body was the stuff of fitness magazines ("Lucky genes, I guess").

But then some bad breaks cracked Lance's porcelain life. In one year, his father's business went belly-up, he crunched his car into a telephone pole, and the biopsy came back positive.

Suddenly, God wasn't behaving like Himself. At least that's the way it seemed to Lance. *Of what use is God,* he wondered, *if my life is as miserable as the next guy's?*

The way Lance figured, he'd be a Christian so long as God lived up to His end of the bargain. But when his good fortune backfired, he bailed on faith.

Like Lance, many believers are conditional Christians. They are enthusiastic when things are cruising smoothly, but when hell hits, they are soon bad-mouthing God for not delivering on His promises.

After all, didn't God say, "[I] will keep you from all harm" (Psalm 121:7, NIV)? Can we not believe the promise that claims, "The LORD will grant you abundant prosperity.

. . . The Lord will make you the head, not the tail. . . . You will always be at the top, never at the bottom" (Deuteronomy 28:11–13, NIV)? And what about this promise: "No harm will overtake you, no disaster will come near your tent" (Psalm 91:10, NIV)?

Does God *really* mean what He says?

Yes, God means what He says. Too many times, however, Christians feast on feel-good promises but ignore texts like John 16:33, "In this world you will have trouble" (NIV). Or consider Psalm 34:19, "The righteous person may have many troubles" (NIV).

Claiming God's promises does not guarantee you an address in the 90210 zip code. Not all Christians are born in Beverly Hills; some live in concentration camps.

In the end, leaning into the promises of God means trusting in the turbulence. It's a choice to live in the hope that all things will ultimately work out well for those who follow Jesus. That's a promise you can bank on.

"For the mountains shall depart, and the hills be removed; but my kindness shall not depart from thee, neither shall the covenant of my peace be removed," saith the Lord that hath mercy on thee (Isaiah 54:10).

Fix this picture firmly in your mind: Jesus, descended from the line of David, raised from the dead. It's what you've heard from me all along. It's what I'm sitting in jail for right now—but God's Word isn't in jail! That's why I stick it out here—so that everyone God calls will get in on the salvation of Christ in all its glory. This is a sure thing:

> If we die with him, we'll live with him;
> If we stick it out with him, we'll rule with him;
> If we turn our backs on him, he'll turn his back on us;
> If we give up on him, he does not give up—for there's no way he can be false to himself (2 Timothy 2:8–13, *The Message.*

"When I suffer, this comforts me: Your promise gives me life" (Psalm 119:50, NCV).

"Let us hold firmly to the hope that we have confessed, because we can trust God to do what he promised" (Hebrews 10:23, NCV).

"I believe the promises of God enough to venture an eternity on them."

—Isaac Watts

"God does not give us everything we want, but He does fulfil all His promises, . . . leading us along the best and straightest paths to himself."

—Dietrich Bonhoeffer

Faith "involves trusting in the future promises of God and waiting for their fulfillment."

—R. C. Sproul

"When our children see us clinging to the promises of God, they will grow up trusting in His goodness."

—Michael Youssef

"Let God's promises shine on your problems."

—Corrie Ten Boom

Greetings, God

Here's what I'm thinking:

Here's what I'm feeling:

Here's how we can do this together:

CHAPTER 16

A Note of Hope

My dear friends,

As you grieve the tragic passing of fellow believers, I hope you do not mourn as people who have no hope. For we share the belief that Jesus died and rose again; therefore, He has power even over death—which is but a sleep, a peaceful pause before the resurrection. God himself assures us that when He comes again, those of us who are alive won't get a head start on those who have died. Actually, they will jump to the head of the line.

What a day it will be! With a command that thunders through the universe and the shout of heaven's chief angel accompanied by a trumpet blast that levels all sound waves, our God will descend through the clouds. Every person who died believing in Jesus will explode out of the grave. The rest of us will join them in the air to meet our Master. Rest assured, this is how we—both the resurrected and the living—will wind up in the presence of our loving Father forever and ever.

Please pass around this note to encourage one another. Spread the hope!

Eternally yours,

Paul, the Apostle

P.S. On that day we'll connect and take a long walk on thin air (1 Thessalonians 4:13–18, The Haff Version).

An old Jewish tale tells of a leper colony that reeked of despair and heartache. Lonely and abandoned men tottered about the yard, waiting to die.

The lepers had no hope—except for one. This man smiled, his eyes sparkled, and his heart still held a song. In this colony of gloom, one man was still human.

Curious about him, the sister in charge wondered what kept him clinging to life in a death camp. Soon, she discovered his secret. Every afternoon at the same time, a woman's bright and smiling face peered over the foreboding wall that circled the compound.

The man waited anxiously to see this woman—the heartbeat of his hope. For a few blissful moments each day, he mirrored her smiles and discreetly waved. Then, he began the long wait to see her again.

One day the sister asked him about the woman. "She's my wife," he said. "Before I came here, she hid me at home. Every day she would smear a magic paste from the native doctor all over my face—except for a spot on my cheek for her to kiss. We knew it couldn't last. Now, she comes to see me every day. And that's why I want to keep living."[1]

In the same way, people of faith can survive (even thrive!) in a world of hopelessness. Of course, we see evidence of despair—gangs, human trafficking, war, crime, fractured homes, terrorism, cancer—but we don't give up. Instead, we lean into faith and share hope with one another.

Brothers and sisters, we want you to know about those Christians who have died so you will not be sad, as others who have no hope. We believe that Jesus died and that he rose again. So, because of him, God will raise with Jesus those who have died. What we tell you now is the Lord's own message. We who are living when the Lord comes again will not go before those who have already died. The Lord himself will come down from heaven with a loud command, with the voice of the archangel, and with the trumpet call of God. And those who have died believing in Christ will rise first. After that, we who are still alive will be gathered up with them in the clouds to meet the Lord in the air. And we will be with the Lord forever. So encourage each other with these words (1 Thessalonians 4:13–18, NCV).

"Be strong and take heart, all you who hope in the LORD" (Psalm 31:24, NIV).

"May the God who gives endurance and encouragement give you the same attitude of mind toward each other that Christ Jesus had, so that with one mind and one voice you may glorify the God and Father of our Lord Jesus Christ" (Romans 15:5, 6, NIV).

"Let us think about each other and help each other to show love and do good deeds. You should not stay away from the church meetings, as some are doing, but you should meet together and encourage each other. Do this even more as you see the day coming" (Hebrews 10:24, 25, NCV).

"Many things are possible for the person who has hope. Even more is possible for the person who has faith. And still more is possible for the person who knows how to love. But everything is possible for the person who practices all three virtues."
—Brother Lawrence

"The hope that God has provided for you is not merely a wish. Neither is it dependent on other people, possessions, or circumstances for its validity. Instead, biblical hope is an application of your faith that supplies a confident expectation in God's fulfillment of His promises. Coupled with faith and love, hope is part of the abiding characteristics in a believer's life."

—John C. Broger

"God never said that the journey would be easy, but He did say that the arrival would be worthwhile."

—Max Lucado

"I would go to the deeps a hundred times to cheer a downcast spirit: it is good for me to have been afflicted that I might know how to speak a word in season to one that is weary."

—Charles H. Spurgeon

"Aloneness can lead to loneliness. God's preventative for loneliness is intimacy—meaningful, open, sharing relationships with one another. In Christ we have the capacity for the fulfilling sense of belonging which comes from intimate fellowship with God and with other believers."

—Neil T. Anderson

---

1. This story is a paraphrase of "The Face at the Wall" in Charles Arcodia, *Stories for Sharing* (Newton, Australia: E. J. Dwyer, 1991), 75.

Greetings, God

Here's what I'm thinking:

Here's what I'm feeling:

Here's how we can do this together:

A Prayer-a-Phrase of Hope

"God of hope, fill me with all joy and peace as I trust in You, so that I may overflow with hope by the power of Your Holy Spirit. Amen" (Romans 15:13, The Haff Version).

God is our refuge and strength,
a very present help in trouble.
Therefore will not we fear,
though the earth be removed,
and though the mountains be
carried into the midst of the sea.

—Psalm 46:1